D1143772

assertiveness

BARRY COLLEGE
LRC

17 MAY

WITHDRAWN
FROM STOCK

TERRY GILLEN

Chartered Institute of Personnel and Development

© Terry Gillen 1997

First published in the *Training Extras* series 1995

First published in the *Management Shapers* series 1998
Reprinted 2000, 2003

All rights reserved. No part of this publication may be
reproduced, stored in an information storage and retrieval system, or
transmitted in any form or by any means, electronic, mechanical,
photocopying, recording or otherwise, without the written permission
of the Chartered Institute of Personnel and Development, CIPD
House, Camp Road, London SW19 4UX.

Design by Curve
Typesetting by Paperweight
Printed in Great Britain by
The Cromwell Press, Trowbridge, Wiltshire

British Library Cataloguing in Publication Data
A catalogue record for this book is available from the
British Library

ISBN
0-85292-769-X

The views expressed in this book are the author's own and
may not necessarily reflect those of the CIPD.

Chartered Institute of Personnel and Development, CIPD House,
Camp Road, London SW19 4UX
Tel.: 020 8971 9000   Fax: 020 8263 3333
E-mail: cipd@cipd.co.uk   Website: www.cipd.co.uk
Incorporated by Royal Charter. Registered charity no. 1079797

contents

Other titles in the series:

introduction

Is this you?

People will look at a book on assertiveness for a variety of reasons. They may have a need to be more assertive and be desperately seeking help; they may know that something is amiss in the way they handle problem situations and be willing to listen to any suggestions that might help; they may already be reasonably competent in the way they handle problem situations but be inquisitive about whether there is anything of value to them in this 'assertiveness' stuff; or they may realise that, at work, traditionally applied authority does not get the best out of people and that, as more and more of us work in teams where we need the help and co-operation of people over whom we have limited authority, an alternative approach is needed. Whatever your starting-point, this book will help. Let me explain how.

How this book will help you

Let us begin with some perspective. If you think of the best boss, colleague, member of staff, friend, neighbour etc, you have ever had and list as many words and phrases you can think of to describe their behaviour when interacting with you, you will discover two things. First, there is no point in making separate lists for each person because you will duplicate most of the words and phrases. Secondly, you will find yourself using words and phrases such as 'open', 'honest', 'straight', 'listens', 'tolerant', 'firm on important issues', 'shows respect', 'confident' etc.

In compiling this list, you will have made an important discovery: these are characteristics that we value in other people irrespective of our relationship with them. It follows, therefore, that other people will value these characteristics in us. In reading this book, you will make another important discovery: these are exactly the characteristics that being assertive will enable you to display. In other words, learning how to be assertive means that you will be someone else's best-ever boss, colleague, member of staff, friend, neighbour etc.

Having gained that perspective, let's now look at some specifics. Have you ever:

- found yourself losing your temper and justifying your lack of self-control by blaming it on the other person? *People like that always make me lose my temper!*

- avoided a discussion with someone else in case it became confrontational, even though it meant it would 'cost' you in some way? *I'm just not very good at handling those situations.*

- held back what you wanted to say because you knew

that if you opened your mouth you'd let the other person have both barrels? *If I'd said what I really wanted to say they wouldn't have recovered for a week!*

● said what you really wanted to say and wished you had not? *Sometimes I can't help myself: I just have to call a spade a spade!*

● feel that other people cause you uncomfortable amounts of stress or dent your self-esteem? *It's just the way I am.*

If you answered yes to any of those questions (and the list is by no means exhaustive – you will find a longer one in the questionnaire in Chapter 1), then you are displaying the characteristics we do *not* value in others, and so you have something to gain from this book.

When people learn how to be assertive, they experience benefits in such areas as:

● handling confrontation more easily and satisfactorily

■ feeling less stressed

▲ having greater self-confidence

● being more tactful

● improving their image and credibility

● being able to disagree more convincingly but in a way that maintains the effectiveness of the relationship

- ▢ resisting other people's attempts to manipulate them through bullying, emotional blackmail, flattery etc

- ▲ feeling better about themselves and other people.

You might want to consider some of these benefits as you formulate your own goals for reading this book.

To help you achieve your assertiveness goals, I have divided the book into five chapters. Chapter 1 will improve your understanding of what assertiveness is and what it is not, and help you establish your goals so that you can get the most out of the book. Chapter 2 explains some of the fundamentals about assertiveness, answering such questions as 'Why do we behave the way we do?' and 'What do we need to do to be more assertive?' Chapter 3 examines the difficult bits of assertiveness, such as controlling your emotions sufficiently well to enable you to maintain control of your behaviour. Chapter 4 shows you how and when to use six assertiveness techniques, and Chapter 5 shows you how to avoid the potential pitfalls when implementing your new-found assertiveness, and answers some common questions.

I have planned your acquisition of the information so that one step leads on naturally to the next. So, unless you are already familiar with the topic, it is very important that you take each chapter in sequence.

Chapter 5 also contains a unique *Learning Log* designed specifically to help you gain maximum benefit from this book. I recommend that you actually copy it onto a larger sheet of paper and, when it is complete, pin it in a place where you will see it every day.

But you could begin the process now. To get the most out of this book, you might want to start thinking about the outcomes you would like (greater confidence, less stress due to the way you react to some people, better interpersonal relations, better resistance to manipulation, higher self-esteem, more credibility etc) and about the situations in which you would like those outcomes, and record them in the appropriate places in the Learning Log (page 73). You might like to do that now.

1 understanding assertiveness

In this chapter we are going to look at:

- four types of behaviour and how to recognise them in yourself and others
- an assertiveness model
- the advantages and disadvantages of the four behaviour types.

But before we do any of that, here is a questionnaire for you (see the table on page 8).

How assertive are you?

If you complete this questionnaire before you read the chapter you will get a more accurate result.

Questionnaire – How assertive are you?

Instruction 1

Score yourself on each statement from 0 to 5, where 0 = 'never or not at all like me' and where 5 = 'always or exactly like me'. Record your score in the appropriate box.

	A	B	C	D
1 When confronting someone about a problem I feel very uncomfortable.	❑			
2 I remain calm and confident when faced with sarcasm, ridicule, or poorly handled criticism.			❑	
3 It's easy for me to lose my temper.		❑		
4 I address problems directly without blame or judgement.			❑	
5 I feel it is all right to ask for what I want or to explain how I feel.			❑	
6 I feel comfortable with the amount of eye contact I make with other people, and I believe they feel comfortable with it too.			❑	
7 I am easily upset or intimidated by ridicule or sarcasm.	❑			
8 It's more important that I get what I want rather than that people like me.		❑		
9 I like it better when people work out what I want without my having to tell them.	❑			
10 I feel confident in my ability to handle positively most work situations involving confrontation with other people.			❑	
11 I'll use the volume of my voice or tough eye contact or sarcasm to get what I want from other people.		❑		

		A	B	C	D
12	I'll use sarcasm or little 'jokes' to make my point.				❑
13	Patience with people is not one of my strong points.		❑		
14	Being liked by people is very important to me, even if that means 'buying' their co-operation at times.	❑			
15	I really don't like conflict and will avoid it any way I can.	❑			
16	I really don't like conflict, so use other ways to make my feelings known such as impatient or 'cutting' by-the-way remarks.				❑
17	I may not be very direct with people but they can tell what I think of them just by looking at me.				❑
18	I find it easy to poke or wag my index finger at other people.		❑		
19	Any impatience I feel for other people comes out in my body language rather than in my telling the other person about it directly.				❑
20	If asked to do something I don't want to do, I'll do it, but deliberately won't do it as well as I could.				❑

Instruction 2

Total your score for each column.   ❑   ❑   ❑   ❑
The higher your score, the more likely you are to
exhibit that behaviour:

Column A = Passive
Column B = Aggressive
Column C = Assertive
Column D = Passive/aggressive

The assertiveness model

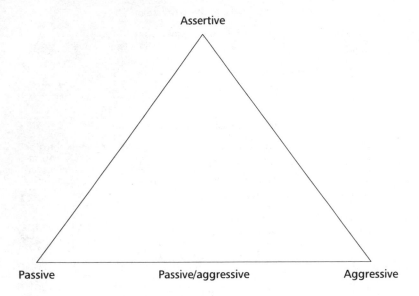

The questionnaire you have just completed will give you a subjective view of the extent to which you exhibit the four behaviour types, so, to satisfy your curiosity, I include a table with descriptions of them (see page 12). As you read them, ask yourself to what extent the description applies to you, highlight the main behaviours you recognise in yourself and also highlight, from the assertiveness description, the ones you would like to exhibit more.

Examining this table you can see, by the behaviours you tend to exhibit, how you are probably perceived by others. It is worth keeping in mind that even if you behave a certain way only 40 per cent of the time, people will perceive you as behaving that way all of the time. So you might like to ask a couple of colleagues to complete the questionnaire about you to get some feedback that is more objective than your own perceptions.

You might be tempted to ask, 'What is wrong with behaving aggressively or passively?' If you are so tempted, consider the following example. The situation is that four different people gave reports of similar size and complexity to four different word processor operators, with instructions that the reports needed to be ready by 3 pm. The time is now 3.15 pm and the reports are nowhere to be seen. Here is how the four different people approached the four word processor operators. As you read the descriptions, imagine the speaker's tone of voice, body language etc.

Passive

Said without much eye contact, in a quiet, hesitant voice and with a lot of fidgeting: 'Hi...er...only me. I hope you don't think I'm being a pain. I know you're awfully busy at the moment, but I was just wondering if that...er...report was...er...possibly...anywhere near ready yet? We've sort of promised we'd try and get it to the...er...customer tonight if that's...er...possible.'

Aggressive

Said with excessive eye contact, leaning over the word processor operator and with a stern expression: 'So where's that *!**! report? I suppose you'll try and tell me you've

The four behaviour types

Behaviour type	Body language	Actions
1 **Passive** Keen to avoid confrontation even at the expense of him- or herself; hopes people will 'know' what he or she wants; excessively concerned with what other people think of him or her.	Minimal eye contact. Quiet, hesitant voice. Rambling speech. Defensive, shrinking posture. 'Hand-washing', fidgeting.	Self-blame. Beats around the bush; avoids the issue. Overjustification; permission-seeking statements. Gives in easily. Generates sympathy; makes people feel guilty in order to get what he or she wants.
2 **Aggressive** Keen to win, even at others' expense; overly concerned with own needs rather than other people's.	Excessive eye contact. Loud, obtrusive voice. Blunt. Expansive posture, invasion of others' space. Finger-wagging and -pointing.	Quick to blame others. Criticises person, not his or her behaviour. Interrupts frequently. Authoritarian. Uses sarcasm, criticism and ridicule to win the point. Makes requests sound like orders. Escalates a situation easily.
3 **Passive/ aggressive** A hybrid behaviour combining passive and aggressive behaviours. Keen to get even without the risk of confrontation.	Minimal eye contact but looking away rather than down. Tight-lipped, impatient sighs. Exasperated or 'I don't believe it' expression. Closed posture.	Indirect responses, sarcastic asides, barbed humour. 'Gets even' indirectly.

Behaviour type	Body language	Actions
3 **Passive/ aggressive** (cont) Often encountered when people want to assert themselves but feel they lack the power to do so.		
4 **Assertive** Keen to stand up for own rights while accepting that others have rights too.	Enough eye contact to let people know he or she is in earnest. Moderate, neutral tone of voice. Moderate, open body posture. Body language congruent with spoken words.	Lots of listening; seeks to understand. Treats people with respect. Prepared to compromise; solution-oriented. Prepared to state and explain what he or she wants. Straight and to the point without being abrupt. Prepared to persist for what he or she wants.

been too busy. It may have escaped your attention but one or two of us have some real work to do. So where the *!* is it?'

Passive/aggressive
Said in a superior and irritable manner within earshot of the word processor operator: 'I suppose if I want that report I'll have to do it myself.' This is followed mentally by 'Next time they want something from me they can whistle for it.'

Assertive

Said in a rational, calm manner with a neutral tone of voice and good eye contact: 'We agreed the report would be ready by 3 pm and it's now 3.15 pm. Is there a problem?'

Notice how it is difficult to take the passive interaction seriously. At best it will generate sympathy and at worst irritability. The aggressive interaction will get people's backs up. Even if this report will soon be ready, future reports will face delays and lack of quality. The passive/aggressive interaction will serve only to irritate. The assertive interaction, however, is the beginning of a rational, non-accusational conversation. After all, if the word processor has crashed or if someone more senior has trumped the report with other work, or if it was more complex to produce than originally envisaged, that is hardly the operator's fault.

Now ask yourself of which person you would prefer to be on the receiving end and what the longer-term repercussions for the four relationships might be. Then take a look at page 15. It shows you the pros and cons of the four types of behaviour.

15

Pros and cons of the four behaviour types

Behaviour type	Advantages	Disadvantages	When appropriate	When inappropriate
1 **Passive**	You avoid confrontation.	You're not taken seriously. Your viewpoint is ignored. You achieve much less than your potential. You suffer self-generated stress. You lose self-esteem. People don't respect you.	When the costs of the confrontation far outweigh the benefits of the possible outcome. When physical violence is threatened.	When the outcome is important.
2 **Aggressive**	You achieve a narrow victory.	You tend to lose in the long term. It irritates and annoys people. People avoid you. People underperform on your issues because they will not use any initiative.	In a crisis when you need people to act without hesitation.	Virtually every other occasion.

(continued on page 16)

Behaviour type	Advantages	Disadvantages	When appropriate	When inappropriate
3 **Passive/ aggressive**	You feel as if you've achieved something, but...	...you haven't. People dislike you, don't trust you and have no respect for you.	Never.	Always.
4 **Assertive**	You achieve results. People like and respect you. Your confidence and self-esteem remain robust. You suffer less stress.	None.	Always, except...	...when the timing is wrong; when the outcome is not worth the trouble.

Review and preview

So, assertive behaviour enables you to stand up for your rights while treating people with the respect they deserve as fellow human beings, colleagues etc. It may not guarantee that you achieve what you want but it does provide three very useful pay-offs:

- ● It gives you the best chance of achieving what you want.

- ◻ It provides the reassurance that you played your part of the conversation positively.

- ▲ It lays the groundwork for effective future interaction.

These pay-offs are needed more than ever. We may live in an age of high technology but we also live in an age when the impact of people on performance has never been greater. More and more of us work in teams in which we need the help and co-operation of people over whom we have no formal authority. Finally, on a broader front, how people feel about us is a direct result of the way we behave towards them, so, the more positive that behaviour, the more valued we are as a boss, colleague, member of staff, or friend.

So, as you behave assertively, remember what I call the *four cornerstones of assertiveness*:

The four cornerstones of assertiveness

Good eye contact	Neutral tone of voice
Open posture	The words you use

Paying attention to these four aspects of your behaviour makes it easier to behave assertively and so reap the benefits and pay-offs described above. Which begs a question: 'If assertiveness is that good, why don't we all behave assertively all of the time?' That, as they say, is the subject of the next chapter.

Before you move on, however, you might like to turn to the Learning Log in Chapter 5 and record in the appropriate section the behaviour changes you would like to make.

BARRY COLLEGE LEARNING RESOURCES CENTRE LIBRARY

2 why we behave the way we do

I hope you noticed something about the last chapter: I never once referred to passive, aggressive, or assertive *people*, but only to passive, aggressive, or assertive *behaviour*. That is because *people* are not passive or aggressive, even though their *behaviour* may be. There is a big and important distinction between a person and a person's behaviour.

You are not your behaviour

Why is this such an important message? There are two reasons. First, if you think of behaviour as something separate from yourself, it is easier to change it; alternatively, if you think about your behaviour as being part of your personality or as something engraved in stone, you may feel it is permanent and so impossible to change. Secondly, separating yourself from your behaviour makes analysing the cause of that behaviour easier. Let's do that now.

In the previous chapter I described four behaviour types. Imagine them as the tip of an iceberg visible above the sea. In this chapter, we are going to look at the massive part of the iceberg concealed from view beneath the surface (see the figure on page 20).

The behaviour iceberg

We shall look particularly at:

○ the behaviour/outcome equation

◻ the 'beneath the surface' sequence of events that 'surfaces' as our behaviour

▲ our natural mechanisms for coping with confrontation and how we implemented those natural mechanisms in childhood and later took what we learnt into adulthood

● what happens when we 'internalise' responses.

In this section you will learn two fundamental lessons for effective interaction with other people: the importance of taking *full responsibility for your behaviour* and what you can do to *take control of your behaviour*.

The behaviour/outcome equation

The behaviour/outcome equation looks like this:

$$S + B = O$$

which means the *Situation* plus the way you *Behave* in it will determine the *Outcome* – see page 22. (Of course, you may not be the only person in the situation, and someone else's behaviour will also affect the outcome, but – and this is a *big but* – your behaviour is the only one you can control. All you can do with another person's behaviour is influence it.) So if you do not like the outcome and you cannot, or prefer not to, avoid the situation, *the only option you have is to change the way you behave in it.*

This is not an easy lesson to learn. Accepting it means that you cannot blame the situation or the other person for the way you behave. You cannot blame the road-hog for making you lose your temper; you cannot blame work pressure for your moodiness; you cannot blame having to see a colleague about an overdue deadline for your nerves. You cannot blame your short fuse, your upbringing, your personality, or the way God made you. It means you take full responsibility for your behaviour.

Once you accept this fundamental lesson you take a major step in becoming more assertive because *now you can gear*

The situation, behaviour, outcome sequence

your behaviour to the outcome you want rather than to the situation you are in.

Having established this fundamental lesson, we can now move on to look at what you can do to take control of your behaviour.

The 'beneath the surface' sequence of events

S + B = O is a valuable lesson in taking responsibility for your behaviour. It does, however, pose two questions: 'Why do different people behave differently when faced with the same situation?' and 'How can I change my behaviour when faced with a familiar situation?' To understand the answers to these questions we need to introduce another element to the equation (see the figure on page 24).

You see, we tend to gear our behaviour more to our dominant feelings than we do to the outcome we want to achieve. This point is so important, I am going to repeat it: *we tend to gear our behaviour more to our dominant feelings than we do to the outcome we want to achieve*. Here are some examples:

Your boss, leaning over your desk, wagging a finger at you as he or she criticises your work, may induce feelings of injustice and powerlessness which cause you to behave passively.

A procrastinating member of staff may induce feelings of frustration which cause you to behave aggressively.

A genuine invitation to explain why a piece of work was not ready at the agreed time may induce feelings of fair treatment and respect which make it easy for you to behave assertively.

The 'trick' to behaving assertively, therefore, is to control your feelings. To help you with that control, we have to answer another question: 'Where do our feelings come from?' In answering that question, we shall have to look at our natural mechanisms for coping with confrontation.

The situation, feelings, behaviour, outcome sequence

Our natural mechanisms for coping with confrontation

Like many other animals on Earth, we have two mechanisms with which we attempt to cope with confrontation: we can *fight* it or we can *flee from* it. This is called the fight-or-flight response. It is an automatic physical response designed to enable us to take rapid action when confronted by physical threat.

As human beings, however, we have another mechanism with which we attempt to cope with confrontation: our *verbal reasoning ability*. This is a deliberate response (ie not automatic) which enables us to communicate our way out of confrontation.

All this sounds pretty straightforward. We use our fight-or-flight response when faced with physical threat and our verbal reasoning ability when faced with emotional threat. And it *would* be pretty straightforward, if it were not for two problems:

● First, our brain seems unable to distinguish between a physical threat and an emotional threat. Most of us, for example, have been caught in a traffic jam and had the experience of increased heart rate, higher respiration rate, a feeling of greater physical strength etc, all of which are fight-or-flight physical responses to a physical threat. Yet the traffic jam is a threat to our emotions, not to our bodies.

■ Secondly, at the time when as children we are learning how to cope with confrontation (our formative years in family and school), that confrontation is with people who are bigger than us (parents, older siblings, school teachers), who make the rules (usually at random, depending on how they feel), and who often behave aggressively or passively towards us in confrontational situations.

And so it happens that during those formative years in which we are learning how to cope with conflict, ask for what we want, express our feelings, and generally relate to other people, we gain more practice during confrontations of using our fight-or-flight response than of using our verbal reasoning ability. In other words, when faced with a situation in which we feel emotionally threatened, we gain more practice in aggressive and passive behaviour than assertive behaviour.

At this stage, there is another question that needs to be answered: 'If that is the behaviour we learn as a child, why do we take it with us into adulthood?'

Internalisation

The answer lies in our having *internalised*, or learnt, the association between the situation and the feelings. Very few situations are completely new to us. We have experienced them, or something like them, before. Even if they seem completely new to us, our brains act as a kind of recognition machine and, spotting something even remotely familiar, interpret the situation for us, tell us what kind of situation it is, and then hit the playback button on our emotional tape recorder. You see, everything that happens to us is mentally recorded and, once recorded, can be played back. And the 'what' that is replayed is the dominant emotion our brain associates with the situation.

In just the same way that the teacher leaning over you criticising your homework triggers emotions of injustice and powerlessness which cause you to behave passively, an aggressive boss leaning over you criticising your work can trigger identical emotions causing you to behave passively in that situation too, because you have learnt to associate the feeling with the situation. The association has become *internalised*. That is, you do not have to think about it: the association is made automatically.

By the time we reach adulthood, many of the feelings we experience in conflicts, and the consequent behaviours, can justifiably be called habit. And in that small word lies a big problem – your robot!

Your robot

To understand what I mean by your robot, I need to describe something about what happens when we learn. Think of a task that was difficult to learn but, once learnt, can be done automatically. Driving a car is an example that will apply to many people. Synchronising the clutch and accelerator, getting into the correct gear, using your mirror properly, positioning the car correctly, watching out for cyclists, not exceeding the speed limit, and checking if you are on the right road take up so much of your conscious thinking that another instruction from your driving instructor causes major panic. Yet in no time at all you are driving along doing everything correctly while continuing a detailed conversation with your passenger. During the learning phase, you have to think about what you do; but once learnt the information is stored in your subconscious and handled automatically.

The thing that enables you to handle such tasks automatically is *your robot*. We all have one. It sits in our subconscious and, once something is learnt, takes over the task. It might be driving a car, photocopying, or knitting – or reacting to confrontation. So once we have learnt to associate feelings, and consequently behaviour, with certain types of situations, we no longer have to think about them: our robot handles the association for us. 'But', you may be thinking, 'why can't I realise that my habitualised behaviour in certain situations is counter-productive, and reprogram my robot?' Well, there is a problem, and it is a bit of a sinister one!

Robots like predictability. They hate change. So your robot does two things to make it more difficult for you to change:

● First, it interprets the outcome of the situation in order to convince you that its programming is correct – see page 29.

■ Secondly, when you try to change your feelings or behaviour, your robot deliberately makes you *feel uncomfortable* in an attempt to convince you that you are wrong and had better revert to your old ways so that you can feel comfortable again. (In Chapter 5, I shall show you how to counteract these moves by your robot.)

How your robot convinces you its programming is correct

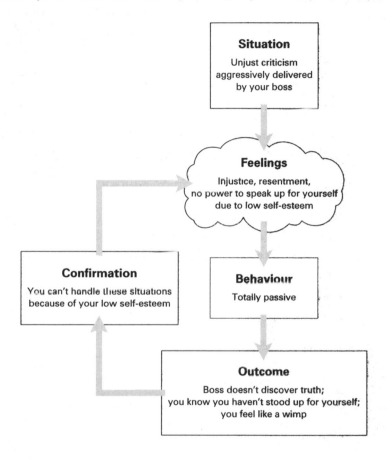

Review and preview

In this chapter we have looked at:

● how vital it is that you take full responsibility for your behaviour. The message is clear: if you do not like the outcome, change your behaviour.

■ how our brains act as a recognition machine and, spotting something familiar in a situation, press the playback button on associated feelings learnt in childhood. We then gear our behaviour to those feelings rather than to the outcome we want.

▲ how our robot handles the association for us automatically and makes it difficult for us to change.

So, in the next chapter we shall look at how to intervene in this process and make it work *for* us rather than *against* us. Before you move on, however, you might like to turn to the Learning Log in Chapter 5 and record points that stand out in your mind.

3 how to think assertively

You will probably have worked out from the previous chapter that *behaving* assertively starts with *thinking* assertively. So before we look at behaving assertively in the next chapter, we are going to look in this one at what you can do to lay the foundations.

I hope you will appreciate the benefits of laying these foundations. If you learn assertiveness at a superficial level it is too easy for your assertiveness to be a bit of an unguided missile. You go around being 'assertive' at any time, in any place, and with anyone, and end up upsetting people, achieving outcomes with consequences you never intended and generally giving assertiveness, and yourself, a bad name. If you lay firm foundations, however, behaving assertively is not only easier, it is more beneficial to everyone concerned and more likely to be sustained.

To help you, we are going to look at:

- your *self-talk*
- your *rights*.

Self-talk

So, what is self-talk and why is it important? Self-talk is the little conversation you have with yourself that stimulates the feelings you associate with a situation. It occurs deep within your subconscious and, as such, is controlled by your robot. Normally, we do not even realise that we have such conversations because the speed of thinking in our subconscious is many thousands of times faster than thinking in our conscious mind. But these conversations, or *inner dialogues*, are there nonetheless.

Self-talk is important for three reasons:

- It is the *earliest point* within the situation/feelings/ behaviour/outcome sequence over which you have control and, hence, the *earliest point* at which you can intervene in the sequence and make it work for you rather than against you.

- Intervening in your self-talk requires *conscious thought*. That is the only way you can begin reprogramming your robot to cause positive, rather than negative, feelings.

- Changing your learnt association between situations and feelings is easier because working with words is more 'tangible' than working with emotions.

Here is an example illustrating how self-talk influences our behaviour and thus the outcome we achieve (see table opposite).

Self-talk and its consequences

	Before	**After**
Situation	Your boss, leaning over your desk and wagging a finger at you, is unjustifiably criticising your work.	Same.
Self-talk	'This isn't fair. Why is the boss always picking on me? I can't even speak up for myself. I feel helpless.'	Criticism may not be pleasant, but if I listen I shall understand why the boss thinks this way and then know how to respond. Anyway, criticism of my work is not criticism of me as a person, even if the boss presents it that way.
Feelings	Powerlessness. Injustice. Inadequacy. Low self-esteem.	OK. Concern that the boss may have misunderstood something.
Behaviour	Passive. Minimal eye contact. Mumbled defensive statements. Self-deprecating remarks.	Assertive. Listening. Acknowledging the boss's concern. Helping the boss understand the facts.
Outcome	The boss thinks he or she is correct. No respect from the boss. Low self-esteem confirmed.	The boss understands the situation correctly. Ground rules for future interaction established. Self-esteem confirmed.

Note. I have kept the example straightforward to illustrate the point, so please avoid the temptation to raise such questions as 'What if the boss is unreasonable?' or 'What if the boss doesn't listen?' Although these questions are perfectly valid (you will find the techniques described in the next chapter helpful in such situations), our focus of attention in this chapter is on what you can control and how you can intervene in the 'beneath the surface' sequence of events to make it work for you rather than against you. So what I hope you notice is how the situation is the same in both examples but how the change in self-talk alters the course of events. And even if, in the 'after' example, the boss had still refused to be reasonable, the ground rules for future interaction would at least have been pointed out to the boss and your self-esteem would still have been intact.

So what I suggest you now do is think of an example for yourself where you behaved passively, aggressively, or passive/aggressively, and construct a table of your own like the table on page 33. As you do so, you will notice how the small change in direction caused by more positive self-talk brings you out at a totally different destination. Before you construct the example, here are two points that will be of help:

● It can sometimes be difficult knowing what your self-talk is. After all, these inner dialogues happen incredibly fast. So be prepared to create one that forms a logical link between the situation and feelings. It may help to imagine you are about seven years old. (If that sounds like a strange suggestion, it may also help to speculate on how many confrontations at work result in the adult equivalent of 'I shan't be your friend any more' or 'It's my ball and I'm going home!')

■ Remember that the outcome includes much more than whether or not one person got his or her way. It includes how you feel about yourself and the other person, how he or she feels about you, whether the relationship has become more or less productive etc.

Having considered your own self-talk, we can now answer another question: 'What can you do to make your self-talk more positive?' That takes us on to the subject of *rights*.

Your rights

Let us look first at what rights are, then at the different types of rights and, finally, at how they can help you keep your self-talk positive.

A *right* is something to which you are entitled. You do not have to qualify for it in any way. There are no preconditions. It is yours 'by right'. In the UK, for example, we have consumer and employment rights. They are the easy ones to identify and to stand up for. The difficult ones are those that are not enshrined in law but relate to how you interact with other people. To help you appreciate these rights and how they can help your self-talk, we shall look at them *generally* and *specifically*.

Here are some examples of *general rights*:

- To be the ultimate judge of your own thoughts, behaviours, and emotions.

- To be treated with respect.

- To state what you want or how you feel.

- To have and express an opinion.

- To be listened to.

- To be imperfect.

- To make mistakes like every other human being.

- To feel OK about yourself.

- To use emotion rather than logic to make some of your decisions if you want to.

- To put yourself first on occasions.

- To choose your own feelings and emotions.

- To stand up for your rights, or not, as you choose.

Let us take a couple of them and see the effect they can have on your self-talk and behaviour (see table opposite).

How rights influence self-talk and behaviour

Right	If you feel you *do not* have the right	If you feel you *do* have the right
To be listened to	You will feel that what you have to say is less important than what other people have to say.	You will feel that what you have to say is as important (no more and no less so) than what other people have to say.
	You will be easily interrupted; your contribution can be easily dismissed; your point of view will be ignored.	You will persist in the face of interruptions and ensure people listen to and understand your contribution and point of view.
		You will also be more inclined to listen to other people.
To choose your own feelings and emotions	You will feel that you have no control over your feelings and emotions, and that situations and other people determine how you feel. It will be easy to adopt a 'victim' mentality.	You will take responsibility for how you feel and have more positive and optimistic thoughts as a result.
		You will be resilient in the face of bullying, emotional blackmail, and flattery.
	You will be easily bullied, emotionally blackmailed, and flattered into doing things which you would prefer not to do.	You will be empathetic with people who are not so emotionally resilient. When you attempt to influence someone else, it will be open and honest influencing, rather than devious.

Thinking of general rights will help your overall understanding. You can make it more specific, however, by thinking also of situational rights. Let's take an example. Your boss wants you to work late tonight to complete a task which has to be ready by 9 am tomorrow. You have a commitment tonight which it is impossible to reschedule. This is how you may see your rights and those of your boss in this situation and how those rights will affect your self-talk and behaviour (see the table on page 40).

Checks on your rights

When thinking of rights, it is all too easy to be unrealistic and stack up most of them in your own favour. You will find it helpful, therefore, to do three things:

● First, always remember that rights carry *responsibilities*. If you want the right to be listened to, for example, you have the responsibility to listen to other people.

■ Secondly, *the other person has rights too*. For example, in discussion with your boss, you may have a right to fair treatment, but your boss has the right to give you straight feedback on your performance or behaviour.

▲ Thirdly, there are three *check questions* you can ask yourself to ensure you have made a balanced assessment of your rights and those of the other person:

○ If you were the other person, would you still feel the rights were fair?

☐ Will the rights you have described lead to positive self-talk and assertive behaviour?

△ Will the outcome be an accurate reflection of both your rights and the other person's?

To help reinforce your understanding of the concept of rights and understand better how to implement it, you might like to try the following exercise: think of two situations where you behaved passively, aggressively, or passive/aggressively and record your rights and the other person's as you see them now, and also describe the behaviour that would be consistent with those rights. You will probably find that the new outcome is very different from the original outcome.

Review and preview

It is easier to behave assertively if you think assertively and, to help you in this chapter, we have looked at:

● how a change from negative to positive self-talk makes it more likely that you will behave assertively

▣ how considering your rights *and* the other person's makes it more likely that you will think assertively.

In the next chapter we are going to look at techniques that make it easier for you to behave assertively. Before you move on, however, you might like to turn to the Learning Log in Chapter 5 and record in the appropriate section points that stand out in your mind about self-talk and rights.

How situational rights influence self-talk and behaviour

Your rights	Your boss's rights	Self-talk and behaviour
None	To make any demand at all and have it carried out; to have staff subordinate their personal lives to work at all times	Powerless to respond; no choice but to concede; subordinate personal needs to those of the boss; concealed resentment towards the boss; poor self-esteem
To work only contractual hours; to put my personal needs first on every occasion	None	'The boss can't make me, so I'll do what I like'; complete refusal and disregard for boss's needs; resentment towards you from boss
To put my personal needs first on occasions	To ask for help beyond contractual hours; to persist in that request	The boss has a right to ask for help but you have a right to set your own priorities in your own time

Listening in order to assess the boss's needs; persistence in explaining your own needs; search for synergistic solution meeting both needs |

4 how to behave assertively

Once you are *thinking* assertively, you will find it easier to *behave* assertively. Assertive behaviour is the focus of this chapter. In it, I am going to show you techniques that make it easier for you to:

- ● stay in control of your feelings
- ■ stand your ground
- ▲ confront an issue with another person.

I shall illustrate the techniques one at a time, because that should make it easier for you to understand them. We shall also look, however, at how the techniques combine in a conversation, because that is how you are more likely to use them. Finally, I shall highlight the points you need to watch for to ensure that you remain assertive and do not inadvertently use the techniques to be aggressive.

Techniques to stay in control of your feelings

Staying in control of your feelings makes it easier for you to behave assertively; the two techniques below help you do that by creating a barrier between you and what someone else is saying – see the figure on page 42.

The emotional barrier techniques

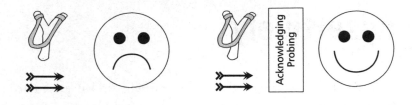

| The slings and arrows of outrageous fortune | Without emotional barrier | | With emotional barrier |

Acknowledging

Acknowledging is a response from you which shows the other person that you heard what they said without it actually affecting your emotions. It has two main uses. The first is in response to a *put-down*. A put-down is a verbal attack on you, sometimes flippant, sometimes concealed behind 'humour' (remember passive/aggressive?), often sarcastic or patronising, and usually totally exaggerated.

Responding to a put-down is a good way to illustrate *acknowledging* as an assertive technique. So, imagine two colleagues talking; Colleague 1 is aggressive and is simply trying to wind the other person up while Colleague 2 (purely to illustrate this technique) uses nothing other than acknowledging. The conversation goes like this (Colleague 2 speaks first):

— Hi, John. Here are the figures you asked for.

— Let's hope they're better than the last lot you cobbled together.

— Yes, let's hope so.

— You must have got the last lot from cloud-cuckoo-land.

— It may have seemed that way.

— You didn't expect my boss to accept them, did you?

— I can understand your boss having difficulty with them.

— Sometimes I wonder if you lot in Personnel work for the same company as the rest of us.

— Sometimes you do.

Now that you have read that dialogue, let me remind you that it was an *illustration* of acknowledging; it is very unlikely that you would have a whole conversation with acknowledging as your only response. What I would like you to appreciate from the illustration is how:

● Colleague 1's attempt to provoke Colleague 2 failed

■ Colleague 2's emotions are totally unaffected by the provocations

▲   difficult it can be, even reading what you know to be a wholly fictitious example, to avoid a passive or aggressive response because your robot is so strongly programmed you want either to retaliate (fight) or defend (flight)

●   responding assertively would gradually educate the first colleague (and it might take months of such 're-education') to stop such unproductive behaviour and replace it with something more open.

Now for the second use of acknowledging. As well as demonstrating that you have heard what the other person has said and keeping your emotions under control, it is a useful way of responding in a non-confrontational manner before moving on. Here is another illustration with the same two colleagues:

-   Hi, John. Here are the figures you asked for.

-   Let's hope they're better than the last lot you cobbled together.

-   You sound as if you weren't happy with the last set of figures.

-   You must have got the last lot from cloud-cuckoo-land.

-   You thought they were unrealistic in some way? Exactly what was the problem?

-   You didn't expect my boss to accept them, did you?

– They weren't what your boss was expecting? Why don't you tell me in detail what your boss said and then we can work out how best to present this set of figures?

– OK, the boss's first objection was…

What I would like you to appreciate from this dialogue is how:

● Colleague 1's attempts at provocation still achieve nothing

■ Colleague 2 acknowledges the *true* or *factual* aspect of what Colleague 1 has said, thus encouraging him, as much as possible, to approach the matter rationally.

This is an important aspect of the second use of acknowledging, because it lets the other person know that you have heard them. Think of what happens when people do not acknowledge. Here is an example: have you ever returned something to a shop because it was faulty, only to be greeted by a shop assistant who tells you, 'No one else has complained'? Ask yourself, does that make you feel better or worse? Would it not have been far better if the assistant immediately acknowledged what you had said?

Probing
Probing is when you make no contribution to the conversation; all you do is 'test' what the other person has

said or seek to understand them better. The first use is excellent defence against a put-down:

- Hi, John. Here are the figures you asked for.

- Let's hope they're better than the last lot you cobbled together.

- What didn't you like about the last set of figures?

- You must have got the last lot from cloud-cuckoo-land.

- Something about the figures felt unreal? What was it?

- What is this, the Spanish Inquisition?

- Does it feel like an inquisition?

- Look, I've got a meeting to go to.

What I want you to appreciate about this dialogue is how:

● the ball is always returned to Colleague 1's half of the court

■ Colleague 2 is not involved emotionally

▲ Colleague 1 has either got to put up (explain the problem) or shut up (back off).

Where Colleague 1 is being flippant and just wants to provoke Colleague 2, probing will probably make Colleague

1 back off, which, in this example, is what he did by retreating to his meeting. Where Colleague 1 has a genuinely felt grievance, however, he is being encouraged to explain it. That is the second use of probing. It gets to the heart of the matter, as illustrated in the next dialogue:

–   Hi, John. Here are the figures you asked for.

–   Let's hope they're better than the last lot you cobbled together.

–   What didn't you like about the last set of figures?

–   You must have got the last lot from cloud-cuckoo-land.

–   Something about the figures felt unreal? What was it?

–   Sometimes I wonder if you lot in Personnel work for the same company as the rest of us.

–   What was it about the figures that causes you to say that?

–   Isn't it obvious? I can see you put a lot of hard work into them but look at the second schedule. With our fixed costs, if we work on a margin of only 8 per cent, as you've suggested, we'll have a negative cash flow by month three. We can't possibly accept that.

Colleague 1 may still be upset about the situation, but at least the conversation has now become more factual. Progress, therefore, is more likely to be made.

Techniques for standing your ground

One of the big problems for people prone to passive behaviour is that they try to be assertive once and, when they are not immediately successful, give in. They do not persist. One of the big problems for people prone to aggressive behaviour is that if they are not immediately successful they quickly escalate a situation. They rub people up the wrong way with remarkable ease. So techniques that help you stand your ground are useful in both sets of circumstances. We are going to look at two: the *three-part sentence* and the *broken record*.

The three-part sentence

The three-part sentence, as the name suggests, is a sentence in three parts. Part 1 reflects what the other person wants. Part 2 communicates how you feel. Part 3 states what you want. Here is an illustration from the two colleagues with the figures.

- Hi, John. Here are the figures you asked for.

- Let's hope they're better than the last lot you cobbled together.

- What was wrong with the last set of figures? I worked very hard putting them together for you.

- Where did you go to get them, cloud-cuckoo-land?

- John, I can see you're concerned about them. However, I feel they were pretty good considering the little time we had to put them together, so I'd like you to tell me exactly what your concerns are.

What I want you to appreciate from this dialogue is how the three-part sentence enables Colleague 2 to:

- reassure John that she understands his position. It is very empathetic. That is crucial because *people listen to us much more easily if they feel we have listened to them.* Reflecting what the other person has said to you (especially in more rational terms than they may have used) is a good way of doing that.

- begin her case by stating her feelings. This has two main benefits. First, sharing our feelings with someone else allows us to come across as open and straightforward; as such, it is seen as a sign of strength. Secondly, no one can disagree with information about your feelings in the way that they might disagree with factual information.

- lay firm foundations for Part 3 which, if delivered on its own, might be interpreted as confrontational.

The broken record

The broken record enables you to stand your ground in the face of bullying, manipulation, and sympathy-seeking. It is one of the most widely used assertiveness techniques. Its effect usually astounds people using it for the first time. It is called the broken record because, just like a scratched record, you repeat exactly the same phrase over and over again. Let's illustrate that with another example: a manipulative boss insisting a member of staff work late.

– Right, John, drop whatever you're doing. I need this by 9 o'clock tomorrow morning. You'll have to stay late. I'm sorry but that's the way it is.

– Sue, if I could I would, but I have to be away by 6 o'clock tonight.

– Whatever plans you've got you'll just have to change them.

– I'd be happy to help any other night, but tonight I have to be away by six.

– Look, maybe you don't realise how important this is.

– I'm sure it is important, but tonight I have to be away by six.

– John, I've promised Accounts that this will be ready first thing in the morning. You're not going to make me break a promise, are you?

– I'll do whatever I can to help, as long as I'm away by six.

– For Pete's sake, John, it's got to be done!

– I'm sure it has and I'll do whatever I can to help, just so long as I can be away by six.

– But you're the best person for the job and I've always been able to rely on you in the past.

– I'll do whatever I can to help, as long as I'm away by six.

- But even if I just give you this bit and I do the other bit it still won't be ready.

- I'll work on it flat out and I'll come in early tomorrow morning, but I'll have to leave at six tonight.

- OK... let's work out how we can get it done.

This is what I want you to appreciate with this example:

● Sue, the boss, is trying all sorts of manipulative tactics to get John, the subordinate, to do what she wants – through bullying, sympathy-seeking, guilt, inducement, and flattery. Yet, as long as John keeps repeating that he has to be away by six, none of Sue's tactics will have any success.

■ John does not have to try to out-argue Sue. As soon as he starts justifying his evening engagement, pointing out how many hours he has worked this week already, or whatever, Sue can begin to out-argue him. The broken record relieves you of the need to be mentally agile!

▲ You can use the broken record to remain completely immoveable or, as John did, to stand your ground while encouraging the other person to shift towards a compromise, and, once that movement begins, relax your position.

● If interactions like this one occur often enough, Sue will learn that the best way to try to influence John is by assertiveness rather than manipulation. John is therefore laying the foundations of a future healthy working relationship with his boss.

Note 1 It is worth making a quick but important point here. Some of you will have read this illustration and thought to yourselves that John should just have told her to take a running jump. If John had done that, he would have achieved the outcome he wanted (leaving at six) but he would also have achieved an outcome he did *not* want (a poorer working relationship with Sue). Some of you, on the other hand, will have been thinking that, where you work, John would have been in trouble for even daring to stand his ground. If John had capitulated at the first request he would have avoided any confrontation, but he would also have suffered resentment towards Sue and, probably, diminished self-esteem. Whereas, in the illustration, they both achieved what they wanted in both the short and the long term.

Note 2 As you relate that illustration to your own experiences, remember that situational rights vary. In one organisation, Sue's action would be reasonable while, in another, it would be unreasonable. So please focus your attention on the dialogue as an *illustration* of the technique and not on whether John would or would not get away with it in your organisation.

Techniques for confronting an issue with another person

Here is another category of techniques. These help you initiate a conversation and, as such, can be more useful when you have to confront an issue with another person. We are going to look at two techniques: *pointing out a discrepancy* and *pointing out a consequence*.

Pointing out a discrepancy

This technique helps you confront an issue with another person in the following sorts of situations:

- where that person has not done something which you had agreed

- where his or her behaviour or performance is below expectation

- where his or her behaviour or performance is outside the norm.

Its benefit is twofold. First, if you are prone to passive behaviour, it gives you a form of words to which the other person cannot react aggressively. Secondly, if you are prone to aggressive behaviour, it prevents you sounding accusatory. Here is an illustration. Bill's punctuality has deteriorated and Sue decides to confront him about it. We shall look first of all at how Sue should *not* handle the situation. In the first illustration, Sue is prone to passive behaviour.

> – Bill, I was just wondering if you could…er…possibly be a little bit more punctual. Creates a bad impression if the boss comes around and people aren't here. You know the sort of thing. Not always easy, I know but if you…well…you know… I'd be awfully grateful.

No doubt you will have noticed that Sue has successfully *diluted* the whole issue so it is unlikely that Bill will give her request much priority. In the second illustration, Sue is prone to aggressive behaviour.

> – Bill. Your timekeeping! Just get your act together, will you? I get it in the neck from the boss when lazy good-for-nothings like you don't bother turning up on time, so just buck your ideas up, OK?

No doubt you will have noticed that Sue has successfully *eclipsed* the timekeeping message with one about her attitude towards Bill. So, even if his timekeeping does improve, their working relationship will suffer. Compare these two illustrations with the third one, where Sue *points out the discrepancy*.

> – Bill, I've noticed that you've started coming in after the official start time. Why is that?

What I want you to appreciate about this illustration is how:

- direct and clear it is

- non-accusatory it is

▲ quickly Sue gets to listen to Bill who may, or may not, have a valid reason for being late

- Sue's credibility as a boss will stay strong. She has addressed a problem directly, but with respect for Bill, not like a bull in an emotional china shop.

Pointing out a consequence

With this technique, you literally tell the other person what will happen if the situation persists. Here is an illustration:

– Bill, I've noticed that you're still coming in after the official start time even though we've spoken about it three times in the past month. Why is that?

– Oh…yeah…sorry, Sue. I'm still having a bit of trouble with the buses.

– Bill, it's your responsibility to get here on time, not the bus company's. I need you here on time, please.

– Yeah…I'll try.

– Bill, that's what you said on the last two occasions. I need something more concrete from you. If you don't come in on time every day next week I'll have to begin the disciplinary procedure. I'd prefer not to do that. Will you come in on time, please?

I hope you will have noticed in this illustration how:

● this technique requires careful handling if it is not to sound like a threat. To ensure that it does not sound like a threat, you should maintain a straight facial expression, keep your tone of voice neutral, and refer back to a preferable option.

■ Sue was factual and precise. There was no '…*might* have to begin the disciplinary procedure'; she would indeed do it, as sure as night follows day, if Bill did not keep to his part of the agreement.

▲ Sue comes across as being totally serious about the issue without having to 'get heavy'.

● the onus of responsibility for his behaviour is exactly where it should be – on Bill.

Putting the techniques together

I mentioned at the beginning of this chapter that I would describe the techniques one at a time because that should make it easier for you to understand them. In real life, however, you are more likely to combine them, so here is a dialogue showing how the techniques can be used together. In this dialogue Sally, one of Bill's colleagues, has approached Bill about his overdue part of a joint assignment:

– Bill, I'm getting anxious about your part of Project X. It was due to be with me the day before yesterday and I haven't seen it yet. Is there a problem? (*Pointing out a discrepancy*)

– Well, I've been kind of busy lately.

– I know you have a lot to do. However, your part of the project is overdue and I can't start my part until I get yours. When will it be ready? (*Acknowledging, probing*)

– I'll get round to it as soon as I can.

Bill, I can't schedule my work until I know when your part will reach me. When will it be ready? (*Broken record*)

– Soon...OK?

– Bill, I know you're busy; however, I'm very anxious about not having the information I need to schedule my work, so I need to know when it will reach me. (*Three-part sentence/broken record*)

– Why is everyone getting at me these days?

– It may seem as if I'm getting at you. But I just need to know when your part of the project will reach me. (*Acknowledging/broken record*)

– Just get off my back, will you?

– Bill, if I can't schedule my work I'll have to explain to Sue that you won't give me a date. I'd prefer not to have to do that. So can you tell me when your part of the project will reach me, please? *(Pointing out the consequence/broken record)*

– Oh, for crying out loud! All right. Let me get my diary.

What I want you to appreciate from this dialogue is how:

● Sally avoided accusations against Bill. She just concentrated on the fact that she had not seen his part of the project and on her need for a date from him. This meant that she also avoided a fruitless conversation about Bill's workload.

■ she avoided Bill's attempts to provoke her ('Get off my back' and 'Why is everyone getting at me?') and stayed focused on her needs while encouraging Bill to be assertive too

▲ Sally's behaviour was geared to the outcome she wanted (getting Bill's part of the project quickly) and not to how she probably felt (thumping Bill for causing her a problem)

● both their rights remain intact.

Note Take great care. When you use these techniques please remember that a slight change in tone of voice or body language will alter the way you come across. What you think is being assertive could easily be interpreted as being aggressive. So, in addition to being aware of 'the four cornerstones' described earlier, I would like you also to be aware of the two tables that follow (see pages 60–62). They highlight when to use the techniques and what to watch for.

Review and preview

In this chapter, we have looked at:

● assertiveness techniques that help you stay in control of your feelings, stand your ground, and confront an issue with someone else

■ how those techniques help you stay focused and not get side-tracked

▲ the importance of applying the four cornerstones of assertiveness if you are to be perceived as assertive.

In the next chapter we are going to look at how you can implement what you have learnt. Before you move on, however, you might like to turn to the Learning Log in Chapter 5 and record in the appropriate section the assertiveness techniques that you feel will help you behave assertively in the situations you have described.

Summary of techniques

Techniques	Description	Use when you want to...
Acknowledging	A response from you that shows the other person you heard what they said without its actually affecting your emotions.	...let the other person know you have heard them; guide them to behave more assertively; control your feelings.
Probing	You question to 'test' what the other person has said or seek to understand them better.	As above plus – you want to get them to 'put up or shut up'.
Three-part sentence	A sentence in three parts which helps you reflect what the other person wants, communicate how you feel, and state what you want.	...encourage them to really listen to your point of view; stand your ground.
Broken record	You repeat the same phrase over and over again.	...remain steadfast on a point; protect yourself from manipulation; encourage them to move towards a compromise.

Techniques	Description	Use when you want to...
Pointing out a discrepancy	You point out to another person where they have not done something which you had agreed, where their behaviour or performance is below expectation, or where their behaviour or performance is outside the norm.	...confront a situation without prejudging it.
Pointing out a consequence	You describe to the other person what will happen if the situation persists.	...convince someone you are serious about taking the matter further but would prefer to reach a satisfactory conclusion; when you need to convince someone to take responsibility for their own actions.

The techniques: what to watch for

Techniques	What to pay special attention to
Acknowledging	Be brief; avoid sounding overly sympathetic or you will come across as patronising; if the other person is particularly emotional, be prepared to paraphrase to avoid emotive words.
Probing	Be brief; avoid long-winded questions that are really several questions rolled into one; maintain an even pace or you will sound like an interrogator; ask genuine questions, not ones designed to trip the other person up, otherwise the conversation will degenerate into a quarrel.
Three-part sentence	Combine the three parts smoothly in one sentence; use 'however' rather than 'but' – it sounds more positive.
Broken record	Avoid appearing intransigent (unless that is really how you want to appear) by suggesting a compromise, but end the suggestion by restating your broken record.
Pointing out a discrepancy	Avoid sounding accusatory by being brief, factual, or descriptive; keep your tone of voice neutral.
Pointing out a consequence	Avoid sounding threatening by being brief, factual, or descriptive; keep your tone of voice neutral; at the end, return to your main goal.

5 your implementation plan

This chapter is intended to help you transfer what you have learnt from this book into sustained behaviour in real-life situations. In it, you will find:

● information to enable you to understand what learning is and how it can be assisted

■ some common questions I am asked about assertiveness and the answers I give

▲ suggestions on how you can continue learning well into the future.

Understanding learning

In this section I am going to give you some information that will help you understand the process you will go through as you become more assertive. Here it is: *when we learn, we go through four stages*, which you will see in the figure on page 65.

Briefly, we progress from not being aware of our shortcomings (Level 1) to being aware of them (Level 2). At these stages, our behaviour is *habit*. The only difference is *awareness*. We then progress to performing correctly but having to think about it (Level 3), otherwise our old habits take over and we 'revert to type' (Level 2). Finally, sometimes after much persistence, we progress to Level 4, where the correct performance is internalised. At this level we have effectively replaced old habits with new ones. It is not until we reach this level that we can say that we have truly learnt what we intended to learn

Now, why is this diagram (opposite) so important? There are two reasons. First, a lot of people stop at Level 2 (conscious incompetence). They know what aspects of their behaviour are counter-productive and what they could usefully change. They delude themselves that just because they are aware of their shortcomings they have rectified them! Secondly, a lot of people experience difficulty at Level 3 (conscious competence). That means you perform the new behaviours but you have to think about them with the conscious part of your mind. And therein lies a problem. Because the conscious part of your mind can only handle one thought at a time, your attention is easily diverted to more pressing matters. That is when your robot takes over (because it does not get reprogrammed until you reach Level 4) and you slip back to conscious incompetence (Level 2).

Your robot makes you feel uncomfortable about this slippage and attempts to convince you that either the change is too difficult for you or that the techniques do not work for you. Either way you can be more comfortable at Level 2 (conscious incompetence) and gradually slip back to Level 1 (unconscious incompetence). That is where your robot is happiest.

Levels of learning

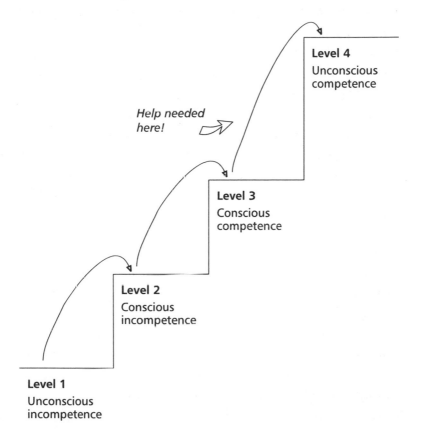

The chances are that, while reading this book, you have reached Level 2 (conscious incompetence) and are ready to have a go at Level 3 (conscious competence). The aim of this chapter is to help you make the journey to Level 4 (unconscious competence).

How to assist your journey to unconscious competence

Your learning log

Practice not only makes perfect, it also helps you progress from Level 3 to Level 4! Persisting with the practice, despite the effort required and despite setbacks, requires motivation. That is why your learning log not only helps you build up the detail of what you intend to implement, it also provides a degree of motivation by pointing out how your learning will benefit other aspects of your life. I strongly suggest, therefore, that the learning log is placed somewhere you will see it regularly.

Self-development

Another recommendation to help you progress from Level 3 to 4 is to engage deliberately in self-development. This is especially important in today's working environment, where lifelong learning is widely recognised as the only effective route to employment security. To do justice to your future prospects, therefore, I have resisted the temptation to summarise self-development in one paragraph. Instead, I would recommend that you use David Megginson and Vivien Whitaker's *Cultivating Self-Development* (see *Further Reading*).

Some common questions

Over the years I have probably been asked thousands of questions about assertiveness. In case there are questions on your mind, I have listed the main ones below together with the answers I give.

1 Does it always work?

Definitely not. Nothing can guarantee that sort of success rate when dealing with people. Assertiveness does, however, give you the best chance of reaching an outcome satisfactory to both parties. And if such an outcome cannot be reached, at least you know that it probably is not your fault, your self-esteem will still be intact, and you will have laid some worthwhile ground-rules for future interaction.

2 Are there any times when I should not try to be assertive?

Yes. When emotions, either yours or the other person's, are running very high. Better to wait for you or the other person to cool off and then start the dialogue.

3 Are there any times when it is OK to be aggressive?

Only one: in a crisis when there is no time for dialogue.

4 Why do people confuse assertiveness with aggression?

Probably because they have been unfortunate enough to come across someone who has learned 'old-fashioned' assertiveness and who goes around asserting themselves irrespective of other people's rights. (See the section on rights in Chapter 3.)

5 How do I make sure I don't come across as aggressive after reading this book?

First, remember the four cornerstones – eye contact, posture, tone of voice, and words – and pay particular attention to tone of voice, because it is very easy, as you try to assert yourself, to sound a little dogmatic or sarcastic. (See the Four Behaviour Types in Chapter 1.)

6 Why is self-esteem so important and how can I improve it?

Self-esteem is the regard in which you hold yourself. Hold yourself in too high a regard and you will probably be self-opinionated, you will not listen to other people, you will interrupt them, and so on. You will be seen as aggressive. Hold yourself in too low a regard and you will probably underestimate yourself and behave passively. Feel 'OK' about yourself and you will find it easier to behave assertively. (See Chapter 3.) Here are six suggestions to help develop your self-esteem:

- Think of yourself as distinct from your behaviour. That way, while you are at Level 2 (conscious incompetence) you will not allow your robot to convince you that getting it wrong now and then is confirmation that you cannot do it.

- Remember that everyone makes mistakes. So learn from them, and above all, don't let them stop you.

- Interpret criticism, no matter how cutting it is, as

someone's opinion and not fact. Criticism is feedback; you have the option what you do with it.

- Resist the temptation to do things you might otherwise not do just because you are concerned about what other people might think of you.

- Be prepared to give yourself priority now and again. Spoil yourself. Be selfish on occasions. Never to do any of these things is you saying that you are not worth it.

- Give your health some priority in terms of both exercise and diet. Aerobic exercise is particularly useful because, after the exercise, the brain releases 'cooling-down' chemicals which induce a sense of well-being and relaxation.

7 What can I do if I just don't feel assertive?

There is a simple but profound answer to this question: *pretend* to be. Let me explain the rationale behind this answer. Your robot likes predictability and stability. It has a vested interest in your staying exactly as you are until the day you die. It will, in short, cause you to underperform. (If you have trouble accepting this statement, ask yourself why is it that people will perform well in a selection interview for a job they do not want and perform poorly in a selection interview for a job they want desperately. Surely, if our conscious mind was in charge, it would be the other way round.)

Our robot resides in our subconscious and our subconscious is incapable of distinguishing between fact and fiction. So if you pretend to feel assertive (and it may take practice), your robot can be tricked into letting you behave assertively. Do that a few times and the positive outcomes reinforce the pretence until feeling assertive is accepted as a replacement program by your robot. Simple, really.

8 How can I prepare for situations in which I need to behave assertively when I am afraid I can't?

Your subconscious is great at visualising. So think of your mind as a video player. Press fast forward, go into the future, and play the forthcoming scene as you want it to go. As I mentioned in the previous answer, however, your subconscious cannot distinguish between fact and fiction. So, if you take charge of your mental video player, you can make it play the forthcoming scene as you want it to go. You still gear your behaviour to your dominant thoughts and experience the self-fulfilling prophecy but, because this time it is positive, it works in your favour. Sportspeople have been doing this for years. It will work for you, too.

9 What if enthusiasm wanes before I reach Level 4? What can I do to keep the pot on the boil?

Here are some suggestions:

● As you read this book, make annotations in it. (Yes, I know: your robot, programmed by successive school teachers, won't like it. So who's in charge?) Underline phrases and points you want to find again, make marginal notes etc. These annotations will make your subsequent reviews of the book quicker and easier.

☐ Review the book and your annotations after a day, a week, a month, three months, six months and a year. From the three-month review onwards, create a new learning log.

10 What is the best way to consolidate what I have learnt? Select two people and, in 20 minutes for each, teach them the main points you have learnt from this book.

Review and preview

In this last chapter we have looked at your learning and focused particularly on what you can do to make the progression from conscious competence to unconscious competence. Please make a note now in the Learning Log of what you will do to reinforce your learning.

Progressing from Level 3 to Level 4 is worth the effort. Look at the outcomes you listed in your Learning Log, and add to them by previewing your future:

○ List three characteristics people will write about you as they describe their best-ever boss, colleague, member of staff, friend, or neighbour. (Feel completely free to pretend you are already totally assertive.)

☐ Remember that, like a pebble creating ripples in a pond, the small changes you implement can have profound consequences, so describe what other aspects of your life will benefit as you become more and more assertive.

Good luck!

Learning log

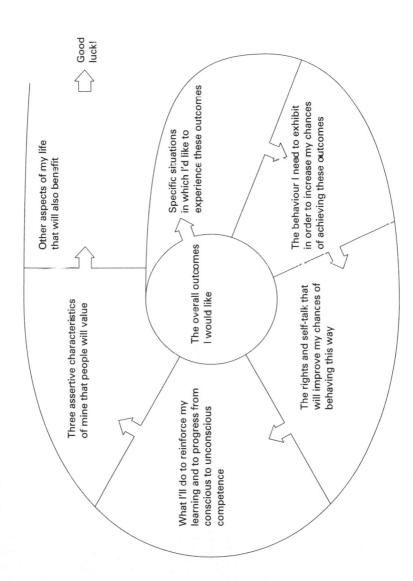

The overall outcomes I would like

Specific situations in which I'd like to experience these outcomes

The behaviour I need to exhibit in order to increase my chances of achieving these outcomes

The rights and self-talk that will improve my chances of behaving this way

What I'll do to reinforce my learning and to progress from conscious to unconscious competence

Three assertive characteristics of mine that people will value

Other aspects of my life that will also benefit

Good luck!

further reading

BLACK J. *Mindstore*. London, Thorsons, 1994.

COATES J. *and* BREEZE C. *Delegating with Confidence*. London, IPD, 1996.

FOWLER A. *Negotiating, Persuading and Influencing*. London, IPD, 1995.

GELLMAN M. *and* GAGE D. *Improve Your Confidence Quotient*. New York, World Almanac Publications, 1987.

GILLEN T. *Agreed! Improve your powers of influence*. London, IPD, 1999.

GILLEN T. *Assertiveness for Managers*. Aldershot, Gower, 1992.

HAUCK P. *How to Be Your Own Best Friend*. London, Sheldon Press, 1988.

HONEY P. *Improve Your People Skills*. 2nd edn. London, IPD, 1997.

KNIGHT S. *Introducing NLP*. London, IPD, 1999.

MACKAY I. *Listening Skills*. London, IPD, 1995.

MEGGINSON D. *and* WHITAKER V. *Cultivating Self-Development*. London, IPD, 1996.

With over 105,000 members, the **Chartered Institute of Personnel and Development** is the largest organisation in Europe dealing with the management and development of people. The CIPD operates its own publishing unit, producing books and research reports for human resource practitioners, students, and general managers charged with people management responsibilities.

Currently there are over 150 titles covering the full range of personnel and development issues. The books have been commissioned from leading experts in the field and are packed with the latest information and guidance to best practice.

For free copies of the CIPD Books Catalogue, please contact the publishing department:

Tel.: 020 8263 3387
Fax: 020 8263 3850
E-mail: publish@cipd.co.uk
View the full range of CIPD titles and order online on the CIPD website:
www.cipd.co.uk/bookstore

Other titles in the *Management Shapers* series

The Appraisal Discussion

Terry Gillen

Shows you how to make appraisal a productive and motivating experience for all levels of performer. It includes:

- assessing performance fairly and accurately

- using feedback to improve performance

- handling reluctant appraisees and avoiding bias

- agreeing future objectives

- identifying development needs.

1998 96 pages   0 85292 751 7

Asking Questions

Ian MacKay
(Second Edition)

Will help you ask the 'right' questions, using the correct form to elicit a useful response. All managers need to hone their questioning skills, whether interviewing, appraising or simply exchanging ideas. This book offers guidance and helpful advice on:

● using various forms of open question including probing, simple interrogative, opinion-seeking, hypothetical, extension and precision etc

■ encouraging and drawing out speakers through supportive statements and interjections

▲ establishing specific facts through closed or 'direct' approaches

● avoiding counter-productive questions

● using questions in a training context.

1998 96 pages   0 85292 768 1

Body Language at Work

Adrian Furnham

If we know how to send out the right body signals, we can open all sorts of doors for ourselves at work. If we get it wrong, those doors will be slammed in our faces. *Body Language at Work* explores how and why people communicate their attitudes, emotions and personalities in non-verbal ways.

The book examines:

- ● the nature and meaning of signals

- ■ why some personalities are easy to read and others difficult

- ▲ what our appearance, clothes and mannerisms say about us

- ● how to detect office liars and fakes.

1999 96 pages   0 85292 771 1

Constructive Feedback

Roland and Frances Bee

Practical advice on when to give feedback, how best to give it, and how to receive and use feedback yourself. It includes:

- using feedback in coaching, training, and team motivation

- distinguishing between criticism and feedback

- 10 tools of giving constructive feedback

- dealing with challenging situations and people.

1998 96 pages   0 85292 752 5

The Disciplinary Interview

Alan Fowler

This book will ensure that you adopt the correct procedures, conduct productive interviews and manage the outcome with confidence. It includes:

- ● understanding the legal implications

- ■ investigating the facts and presenting the management case

- ▲ probing the employee's case and diffusing conflict

- ● distinguishing between conduct and competence

- ● weighing up the alternatives to dismissal.

1998 96 pages   0 85292 753 3

Introducing NLP

Sue Knight

The management phenomenon of the decade, neuro-linguistic programming (NLP) provides the techniques for personal growth. Use it to develop your credibility potential and value while also learning to excel at communication and interpersonal skills.

The author looks at:

- the essence of NLP and how it can work for you

- using NLP to achieve what you really want

- how to build quality relationships and enhance your influence in the workplace.

1999 96 pages   0 85292 772 X

Leadership Skills

John Adair

Leadership Skills will give you confidence, guidance and inspiration as you journey from being an effective manager to becoming a leader of excellence. Acknowledged as a world authority on leadership, Adair offers stimulating insights on:

- recognising and developing your leadership qualities

- acquiring the personal authority to give positive direction and the flexibility to embrace change

- acting on the key interacting needs – to achieve your task, build your team and develop its members

- transforming such core leadership functions such as planning, communicating and motivating into practical skills that you can master.

1998 96 pages   0 85292 764 9

Learning for Earning

Eric Parsloe and Caroline Allen

Today, lifelong learning is a must if you want to get onwards and upwards, and if you don't take charge of your own learning, then, frankly, no one else will. *Learning for Earning* shows exactly how to set about doing this.

The authors examine:

- using interactive exercises, quizzes and games to get you thinking

- how to reflect on what you have read and relate it to your own situation

- how to use other sources of information – people, organisations – to help you

- the use and benefits of 'action promises' – the actions you intend to take after reading.

1999 96 pages   0 85292 774 6

Listening Skills

Ian MacKay
(Second Edition)

Improve your ability in this crucial management skill! Clear explanations will help you:

- ◉ recognise the inhibitors to listening

- ◼ listen to what is really being said by analysing and evaluating the message

- ▲ interpret tone of voice and non-verbal signals.

1998 80 pages   0 85292 754 1

Motivating People

Iain Maitland

Will help you maximise individual and team skills to achieve personal, departmental and, above all, organisational goals. It provides practical insights into:

- becoming a better leader and co-ordinating winning teams

- identifying, setting and communicating achievable targets

- empowering others through simple job improvement techniques

- encouraging self-development, defining training needs and providing helpful assessment

- ensuring that pay and workplace conditions make a positive contribution to satisfaction and commitment.

1998 96 pages   0 85292 766 5

Negotiating, Persuading and Influencing

Alan Fowler

Develop the skills you need to manage your staff effectively, bargain successfully with colleagues or deal tactfully with superiors. Sound advice on:

- probing and questioning techniques

- timing your tactics and using adjournments

- conceding and compromising to find common ground

- resisting manipulative ploys

- securing and implementing agreement.

1998 96 pages   ISBN 085292 755 X

Working in Teams

Alison Hardingham

Looks at teamworking from the inside. It will give you valuable insights into how you can make a more positive and effective contribution – as team member or team leader – to ensure that your team works together and achieves together. Clear and practical guidelines are given on:

- ● understanding the nature and make-up of teams

- ◻ finding out if your team is on track

- ▲ overcoming the most common teamworking problems

- ● recognising your own strengths and weaknesses as a team member

- ● giving teams the tools, techniques and organisational support they need.

1998 96 pages   0 85292 767 3

BARRY COLLEGE
LRC

17 MAY

WITHDRAWN
FROM STOCK